Bring on the SWORD!

Dana White

GReaT S✳uRCe®
EDUCATION GROUP
A Division of Houghton Mifflin Company

CO-ASC-100

Reading Advantage Authors
Laura Robb
James F. Baumann
Carol J. Fuhler
Joan Kindig

Project Manager
Ellen Sternhell

Editor
Jeri Cipriano

Design and Production
Preface, Inc.

Photography and Illustration
Front cover, p. 29 © Le Segretain Pascal/Corbis SYGMA; pp. 1, 33 © AP
Photo/Massimo Sambucetti; p. 6 © Yann Arthus Bertrand/Corbis; p. 9
© Al Messerschmidt/WireImage.com; p. 13 © 1998 Zorro Productions, Inc./
© 1998 TriStar Pictures, Inc.; pp. 17, 18, back cover © DK Images; p. 23
© AP Photo/Diane Bondareff; pp. 26, 48 © Victor Spinelli/Wireimage.com;
p. 32 map art by Sue Carlson; p. 34 © Wally McNamee/Corbis; p. 38
© Robert Brenner/PhotoEdit; p. 41 © Phil Schermeister/Corbis; p. 42
© Brian Bahr/Getty Images; p. 44 © Ezra Shaw/Getty Images; p. 45
© Chris Trotman/NewSport/Corbis

Printed in the United States of America

International Standard Book Number: 0-669-51403-9

2 3 4 5 6 7 8 9 10 -RRDC- 09 08 07 06 05

CONTENTS

1

Pan American Games— March 12–17, 1995

"Fencers ready," the referee says.

"Yes, ready. Fence," Peter Westbrook replies. He is 42 years old—old for competitive fencing. Most fencers retire at 34. He has been back in training only since last fall. Then, his coach, Csaba Elthes, urged him to try to compete in the 1995 Pan American Games.

Westbrook thought it was a bad idea. He had been semi-retired since the 1992 Olympic Games in Barcelona. At that time, he had been a member of the United States fencing team, but he had not even qualified for individual events. He had not been one of the top two fencers in qualifying bouts.

More importantly, he no longer needed medals or titles to be somebody. He was already a fencing legend. Why bother making a comeback?

But Elthes kept pushing. He accused Westbrook of being lazy, of going soft.

Westbrook found it hard to ignore Elthes's pushing. Westbrook and his coach were very close. After all, they had worked one-on-one for many years.

Westbrook talked it over with officials of the United States Fencing Association (USFA). They said he had not been training. Fencing rules had changed. He should step aside for a younger man.

That did not sit right with Westbrook, so he trained hard. And he qualified as an individual fencer. And he was given the honor of carrying the U.S. flag at the opening ceremonies of the 1995 Pan American Games.

Mar del Plata, Argentina, was the site of the 1995 Pan American Games. Athletes from North America, Central America, South America, and the Caribbean participate in this competition, which is the second largest next to the Olympics.

The Match Begins

So, here Westbrook is on the *piste,* the narrow strip of matting that is fencing's playing field. He wears a full head mask; his metallic *lamé,* or jacket; gloves; and tights. Saber in hand, he faces a sneering opponent, a man who had taunted him.

"Yes, ready. Fence!" says Westbrook's opponent, Arjistedes Faure.

Faure is a black Cuban, 6 feet 4 inches. Everyone calls him Fabio. He is young and has defeated Westbrook in the past. Worse, on the practice strip in the last few days, he defeated the whole U.S. team, including Westbrook! Now, Fabio looks confident, very strong.

"En garde!" says Fabio. This is French for *on guard,* "get ready." Most fencing terms are in French.

Westbrook swallows his nervousness. He adopts a confident air and says a quick, mental prayer. He begs God to help his saber work magic and to put him "in the Zone"—a mental space where he will feel great power.

Fabio attacks—a *thrust.* Westbrook blocks—a *parry.* Then Westbrook counterattacks—a *riposte.* He scores a *touch*—a point. He leads, 1–0.

The two back off—a *remise*. After a fencer scores a point, they stop and start over again.

Fifteen touches (points) is a *bout*. The scores of contest bouts are usually close—15–14, for example, or 15–12. A score of 15–11 is considered an excellent score for the winner.

Westbrook and Fabio start another *phrase*. Fencing is musical as well as graceful. A completed series of actions—thrust, parry, riposte, remise—is a phrase.

Westbrook scores again. Now, it is 2–0.

Fabio is setting a quick tempo, or rate of attacks or reactions. Fencing action can look like a blur to people unfamiliar with it. It is scored electrically. Wires in the fencers' clothes register touches.

But inside that blur are superior footwork and coordination and great physical strength. And, perhaps more important, a quick mind. A great fencer can predict an opponent's next move. Fencing is like playing chess with your body three or four moves ahead.

Soon, the score is 5–0. Then, suddenly, Fabio scores to make it 5–1.

Westbrook goes on the attack. He can see and

smell Fabio's fear. He gets touches six, seven, and eight and keeps on attacking. He keeps making the right "choice in time."

"In the Zone"

Westbrook's prayer has been answered. His saber is magic. "I let him feel my power," Westbrook writes in his autobiography, *Harnessing Anger.* "I let everybody in the whole audience feel my power. I let the officials feel my power."

Westbrook is "in the Zone." He eventually wins 15–5. This is an upset. The audience gapes, astonished.

Westbrook received the gold in men's saber at the 1995 Pan American Games. His focus helped him succeed.

Westbrook's triumph brought respect from Fabio. USFA officials did an about-face, telling Westbrook they always knew he could do it. Reporters who had asked, "Are they letting just any old body carry the flag in the opening ceremonies?" ate their words. It was a historic comeback for Peter Westbrook.

CHAPTER

2

Why Fencing?

Almost from the moment he was born, Peter Westbrook had to be on guard. He grew up in Hayes Homes Projects in central Newark, New Jersey. There were twenty or so buildings in the project, each twelve stories high. Westbrook later called it an "urban reservation for poor people." There was television, but no real contact with the world.

When Peter was eleven months old, his sister Vivian was born. Their mother, Mariko, was Japanese. She had fallen in love with their father, an African American soldier named Ulysses Westbrook. They were married in Japan. Her wealthy family disowned her. They would not have accepted anyone who was not Japanese. Even in the United States at that time, racially mixed marriages were uncommon.

The Westbrooks' marriage was not a good one. Finally, they separated, but they did not divorce.

Divorce was against Mariko's religious faith. Her family was one of the few Catholic families in Japan.

Growing Up in New Jersey

So Mariko became a single parent in a foreign country. She did not have a job. They were poor. Holes in the kids' shoes were filled with cardboard. But she held fast to the values of self-discipline, good manners, and a good heart.

Mariko also believed in education. She wanted her son to get a Catholic education. The tuition was far beyond her means. She begged officials of St. Peter's Catholic School to let Peter attend school there for free. In exchange, she promised to work at whatever was needed.

The school officials said no at first, but she kept asking until they gave in. She cleaned the priests' rectory, served drinks at bingo games, and did whatever else was needed. Vivian entered school the year after Peter on the same basis.

School was a haven for Peter. The black nuns were as strict as his mother. But he formed warm relationships with them.

Life in the Hayes projects became worse over time. Being half-Asian, Peter and Vivian were targets for racial teasing. Peter learned that getting beaten up by a gang of kids was no excuse to go crying to his mother. Losing a fight might earn a slap from her. She knew he had to be stronger to survive.

Peter found a hero on television—Zorro. The Latino hero was a masked defender of justice, a people's hero like Robin Hood. Zorro rode his horse into trouble and fixed problems with dazzling swordplay. Then Zorro would leave his mark, using three strokes of his saber—*shoup, shoup, shoup!* It made a burning "Z."

Many movies and books have told of Zorro's adventures.

Peter dressed like Zorro on Halloween. He even carved a "Z" on his mother's coffee table. She didn't punish him for scarring the furniture. But she punished him when she caught him pitching pennies for change. His mother ran up and slapped him hard in front of his friends.

Peter did not like that. Nor did he like his mother ordering him around or telling him what to wear. When he was fourteen, he moved in with his father and the woman living with his father.

About three months later, Peter came home one day to an empty apartment. He found the bag of clothes he had brought with him in a closet. His father had left twenty dollars and a note saying that he would be in touch.

The woman whom Peter's father was living with had a sister. Peter moved in with the sister. His mother phoned often to tell him to come home, but Peter at first refused. His father finally did phone to ask if he wanted to come live with him in Florida. Peter said he was going back to live with his mother, which he did.

By now, Mariko had a regular nine-to-five job at a factory. Money problems eased a little. But her discipline did not.

The Way of the Warrior

Peter started boxing in the Police Athletic League and fighting in the streets. Mariko felt she had to stop him somehow from those fistfights. She told him about the samurai tradition in their family.

In Japan, the samurai were the fearsome warriors from the upper class. Their duty was, first, to serve the emperor, and second, to serve everyone else. The samurai followed a code of conduct called *Bushido*. They valued honor above life. Honor was made up of loyalty, compassion, and integrity. *Integrity* means taking responsibility for everything you say or do.

A samurai's soul was said to be in his or her sword. The sword was a battle weapon. It was also a necessary part of spiritual growth.

Mariko did not see the great purpose or the philosophy of the samurai in fistfights. She wanted her son to take up fencing. She thought he would meet a more noble class of people.

Peter was not impressed with his mother's samurai stories. And he thought fencing was a "strange white sport." But he agreed to try it when Mariko said she would give him five dollars for every fencing lesson he took. That was convincing!

CHAPTER

3

Why a Saber?

The place where Peter took fencing lessons was Essex Catholic High School. It was only two bus rides from his neighborhood, but it was a very different world. Essex High was a mostly white, all-boys' school.

Training at Essex High took place after school from 3 to 6 PM. Its athletic program had been the training ground of Olympic-level competitors. Fencing was one of the school's strongest athletic programs.

Samuel D'Ambola, a medical doctor, started the fencing program because he liked young people, and he liked the sport. He sized up young Peter Westbrook and handed him a saber. Fencers often begin with a foil, but the saber turned out to be a wise choice for Peter.

The Weapons

Three weapons are used in the sport of fencing. These are the *foil*, the *épée* (ay PAY), and the *saber* (sometimes spelled *sabre*). Fencers usually specialize in one weapon. But they can compete in events of all three weapons if they wish.

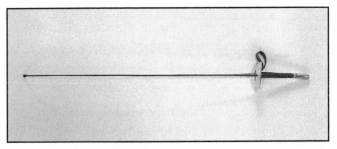

Foil

The foil's flexible, rectangular blade is about 35-inches long and weighs less than a pound. Poking with the tip of the blade scores points. The touch must be in the opponent's target area, which is the torso from shoulder to groin, front and back. The neck, arms, head, and legs are invalid targets.

Points are scored electrically. The fencer, called a *foilist*, wears a metallic jacket *(lamé)*. Wires in the lamé connect to a machine. When the tip of the foil hits the jacket, the machine scores a point.

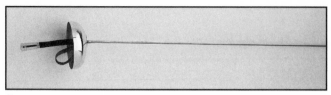

Épée

The épée is a descendant of the dueling sword. The object of serious duels was to run your blade through your opponent's body. The blade is the same length as the foil, but it is stiffer. The épée is heavier than the foil, weighing about 27 ounces. Its guard is much larger than the foil's. This part protects the hand from a valid touch.

The fencer, an *épéeist,* can only use the tip of the blade to score a touch, but the entire body is the valid target area. Points are scored electrically.

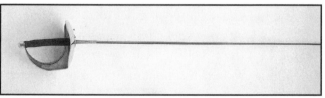

Saber

The saber is the modern version of the cavalry sword. Zorro used a saber. So did pirates. The saber is similar in length and weight to the foil. But the fencer—called a *sabrist* or *sabreur*—may slash and cut as well as thrust, or poke.

The target area is from the bend of the hips, front and back, to the top of the head. This is similar to the target area of a mounted cavalry fighter. When many countries had cavalries (soldiers on horseback), the object of swordfighting was to take out the cavalryman but save the valuable horse.

The fencer's uniform includes a metallic jacket (*lamé*) and a mask with a metallic covering to protect her or him from head slashes. Points are scored electrically.

The Right Choice of Weapon

Fencing is a combat sport. All fencers are fighters. But they fight in different ways. Peter attacked and fought with his fists. A fencer using a saber fights in a similar attacking style. So that's why Dr. D'Ambola chose the right weapon when he handed Peter a saber.

Peter had had plenty of experience slashing and slinging with sticks, rocks, and bottles. With a saber in his hand, he felt like Zorro. Saber fencing was like street fighting—but his mother approved. She was also happy that training kept Peter off the streets. Traveling to competitions took up even more of his free time.

Within weeks, Peter was able to beat eighty percent of the other students in the fencing program. Soon, he was the top man. As a junior and senior, he was the captain of a powerful team. That felt great.

Peter's family's move from the projects to the suburbs also felt good to him, for the most part. They rented a floor in a relative's house. There was grass and space. But there was also a new situation and a lot of uncertainty.

New Moves

In Peter's new neighborhood, it was "better" to be Asian than black. He wondered if the other kids knew how poor he was. People here were so quiet and private. Sometimes, he felt uncomfortable and lonely. Sometimes, he went back to his old neighborhood to hang out.

But fencing kept Peter focused. And he was learning the new suburban rules. His mother's insistence on good manners was paying off. Kids accepted him. He dealt with those who did not accept him by using the rules of his old neighborhood. But mostly, he focused on being the best high school fencer in the state—and he was.

Being a top fencer led to another move for Peter. New York University (NYU), in New York City, sent Peter a letter. NYU had a fine college fencing team, and they wanted Peter.

Mariko wanted him to go to college. And several of Peter's high school friends were going to NYU. So Peter decided to follow the crowd and see what developed. After all, he would be fencing for NYU!

CHAPTER
4

College, Confusion, and a Coach

A full scholarship left Peter Westbrook free of money worries. But there were other challenges. It was 1970, and U.S. troops were fighting in southeast Asia. Demonstrations against the war in Vietnam filled the route from Peter's apartment in Greenwich Village to NYU. There were more demonstrations on campus.

It was a very troubling time for everyone, especially college students. Westbrook often felt overwhelmed. Once again, he was facing different social rules. He was lucky to find a friend who suggested he see therapist Mildred Klingman.

Throughout the 1970s, Dr. Klingman helped Westbrook understand his feelings. He began to lose his fears and insecurities. He started being open to new experiences rather than prejudging them.

Fencers learn the positions for fencing first without any weapons in hand. Training like this helped Westbrook in many ways.

Coach Csaba Elthes and Winning Times

Westbrook had two things going for him—therapy and fencing. During his junior year, NYU coaches suggested he start training with Csaba Elthes, a Hungarian sabrist at the New York Fencers Club.

Elthes had escaped to the United States during the Hungarian Revolution of 1956. He had the reputation of being the best coach in the country. He also had a rough manner. Sometimes, he would hit a student with his sword. It was not unusual for students to leave bleeding from lessons with Elthes.

Westbrook put up with this for a semester. Then he wondered why he should pay someone to abuse him. He left his coach.

But Westbrook continued fencing. He won his first big title in 1973—the National College Athletic Association (NCAA) championship. He was the best college fencer in the country. And he loved it!

As unpleasant as training with Elthes had been, the man had helped Westbrook. Now, Westbrook wanted to be on the U.S. Olympic team. For that, he needed a coach. And he knew that he could not find a better one than Elthes.

So, a year after Westbrook had quit training with Elthes, Westbrook went back to his coach. They began a grueling schedule. Westbrook trained seven days a week from 4 PM to 9 or 10 PM each night. Elthes still hit other students, but he no longer hit Westbrook.

Elthes paved the championship road for Westbrook in another important way. He pointed out how necessary it was to get along with the right people. The politics of fencing was tricky to begin with. It was even more so for an African American at this time since the referees were white. They were the ones who decided whether to score a touch because saber bouts were not yet scored electrically then.

Westbrook appreciated Elthes's advice. But Westbrook also felt that nothing could stop him. And, in fact, the list of his wins during the next two years was great.

In 1974, as a college senior, Westbrook was U.S. National Champion, men's saber. (He would win this title thirteen times! This had never been done before.) The same year, he was a member of the U.S. World Championship Team.

In 1975, Westbrook won a bronze individual medal at the Pan American Games. He also helped bring home a team silver medal that year. Again, he was U.S. National Champion and a member of the U.S. World Championship Team.

From youth to adulthood, Westbrook has always been a fighter.

Unexpected Losses

However, two things that happened later in 1975 made Westbrook think that he really should quit fencing. First, he lost the 1975 Pan American gold medal by one point. Second, he lost the 1976 National Championship. This was not meant to be one of his "lucky thirteen" wins. Worse, he lost to a fencer who was a favorite of Elthes and whom Elthes wanted to win.

Devastated, Westbrook shut down emotionally, but he went on fencing. He was looking almost desperately for the next win. *That* would tell him he was worth something.

CHAPTER

5

Olympian!

Westbrook's mood was dark and jumbled as he went off to Montreal, Canada, in 1976. He was twenty-four years old. It was his first Olympics. He was intimidated by the mass of superstar athletes there. He was also uncomfortable with the attention he was receiving.

People were watching Westbrook because he had placed number two in the world in pre-Olympic trials. Earlier, he had beaten several top Europeans to win an international fencing challenge. But Westbrook felt like he did not belong there. Some world champions asked him to spar with them. He felt that they were trying to see how good he was. But he still could not accept his ability.

On the practice strip four days before his event, Westbrook injured himself. Doctors said he could not compete. It was a relief. Even if he went against the doctors' advice, he could not be expected to win.

Fencing and Life

Westbrook competed and came in thirteenth at the 1976 Olympics. He was pleased with his results. The next year, he won back the U.S. national title—and held it for the next eight years.

The United States boycotted the 1980 Olympics. Instead of going to Moscow, the U.S. team went to China. For three weeks, they traveled and competed against China's best teams. Westbrook was the only team member who went undefeated.

Two sabrists in action

Yet Westbrook still felt insecure about his fencing ability. He needed those wins to feel good about himself. Fencing was his obsession. Nothing else mattered. And nothing in fencing mattered so much as winning.

Westbrook had become an expert at reading people. He beat them by preying on their weaknesses. This makes for a great fencer. But being combative does not work well in the outside world.

Westbrook, like many U.S. fencers, had to work for a living. Fencers from other countries are often paid *subsidies,* or money from the government. Fencing is their job. But in the United States, fencing is not yet a spectator sport. Money is showered on basketball, football, and baseball players here. But U.S. fencers are not household names. None has ever been named Athlete of the Year as European fencers have.

Westbrook graduated from college with a degree in business. Armed with that degree, he went to work for IBM. He sold computers. He stuck it out at IBM for three years. He went to work at two other companies over the next twelve years. At quitting time every day, he ran to the fencing club to train. Corporate America was where he earned his living. The fencing strip was where he *lived.*

After working for years, Westbrook had more money than he could spend. He had a lot more fencing titles, too. He had success and a certain amount of fame. But he did not feel "full." There had to be some bigger purpose to life.

So began Westbrook's search to understand himself better, his anger, and his life. His quest would continue through to his winning the gold medal in the 1983 Pan American Games in Caracas, Venezuela. By the 1984 Olympics in Los Angeles, California, he had found a few answers.

The answers helped him work "in the Zone" and challenge unfair calls. He won a bronze Olympic medal. Winning it told him something new. If he could win against champions from all over the world, he could use his emotions and win against obstacles in life.

Westbrook began to use his anger as a fuel in competitions. Anger gave him focus and energy. Also, he now began to learn how to turn the anger off when he pushed up his mask and stepped off the piste.

So, his loss at the 1987 Pan American Games three years later did not destroy him emotionally. He no longer thought he had to win to be somebody. He finally was at peace with himself.

There were more good things to come. Westbrook met and married Susann Miles. He went to live in Harlem with her and his stepson, Dorian. He also rediscovered his roots there. All his life, Westbrook, who is part-African American and part-Asian American, had denied his Asian heritage. But Japanese relatives traveled around the world to attend his wedding. In accepting life, Westbrook found a lot to embrace. He even joined a Baptist church that continues to inspire him.

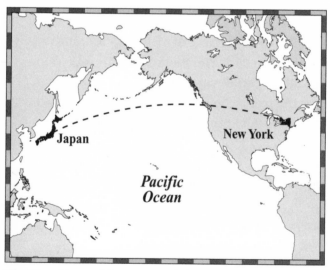

Westbrook's wedding was a time to reconnect with his family and heritage. His Japanese relatives traveled a long distance to celebrate with him.

The Olympics

The 1988 Olympics in Seoul, Korea, brought even more breakthroughs for Westbrook. For the first time, five African American fencers competed together. Westbrook and fellow sabrists Mike Lofton and Bob Cottingham were there from the New York Fencers Club. There were also foilists Peter Lewison and Sharon Monplaisir.

The 1988 Summer Olympics in Seoul, Korea, represented a new era in fencing.

Sharon Monplaisir had to overcome many hurdles to reach the 1988 Summer Olympics.

Monplaisir's history echoes Westbrook's. She grew up in New York City's tough South Bronx area. A high school fencing coach introduced her to fencing. She brought her own dedication to the sport.

Once considered a pastime of the privileged, the face of Olympic fencing has changed. No longer are all the faces behind the masks white. They are also no longer all male. There have always been women fencers—women samurai, swashbuckling pirates and privateers, duelists, and entertainers. But women Olympic fencers are a fairly recent thing.

Fencing is the only combat sport in which women can compete in the Olympics. The first Olympic women's fencing event was in 1924. Not until 1996 was there a women's Olympic épée competition. The 2004 Olympics in Athens, Greece, was the first time women sabrists could compete.

CHAPTER

6

The Peter Westbrook Foundation

Westbrook became a six-time Olympian in 1996. He dedicated that competition to his mother and Csaba Elthes. Both had died. Westbrook also became a fencing legend. No U.S. fencer has brought home an Olympic medal in fencing since he did.

Westbrook also has accomplished something else that is just as important to him—the creation of the Peter Westbrook Foundation. It was launched in February 1991. He wanted to advance what he calls fencing's "grassroots urban" expansion. In many places, there were *salles* (sals), or fencing clubs. But there was nothing for inner-city kids.

Having the kids learn life skills was a priority for Westbrook. He wanted the kids to learn how to win or lose, deal with stress, control emotions, and strive for excellence. He felt that all of these skills could be developed through fencing.

Starting Out

Westbrook started with three partners, a board of directors, and a coaching crew. His partners were all African American, college-educated men. On the board of directors were a former NYU president and champion athletes, such as Wilma Rudolph and Arthur Ashe.

Only six kids came to the first Saturday morning session at the New York Fencers Club in downtown Manhattan. The next week, however, there were forty kids of many different races.

Soon, there were seventy-five kids. The kids piled in eagerly, practiced calisthenics and footwork drills, listened to short lectures or guest speakers, or watched instructive films. They talked about schoolwork and discussed essays from a bimonthly contest. Then, they did what Westbrook calls the "cheese"—flashy swordplay.

More kids wanted in on the three-hour sessions. Soon, there were one hundred kids, ages nine to seventeen. Some traveled over an hour to get there. "Bring on the swords!" they said. "Bring on the coaches!"

Students practice their fencing skills for long periods of time.

Early on, Olympic coaches Csaba Elthes and Aladar Kogler had asked to be part of the program. Then, foilist Eric Rosenberg brought over his ten students and his assistant, Olympic prospect Herby Raynaud. More Olympic-level coaches were added—Cuban and Afro-Cuban, Ukrainian, Russian, and Haitian. All these nations are fencing powerhouses.

Working On

The plan for the foundation is simple. Let the kids belong to something positive. This is the family and community of the salle, the fencing club. Show the kids what it takes to remain a part of the salle—finishing schoolwork, writing essays, committing to the discipline of the work, and facing their fears.

"My job," Westbrook says, "is to transform [the kids], to create great kids, great citizens, academic scholars. And also the icing on the cake is to create world-class athletes."

The heart of a samurai warrior is in that statement. There is also the heart of a legendary fencer from the New Jersey projects.

CHAPTER

7

Westbrook's Warriors

Westbrook motormouths his way through Saturday morning's sparring kids: "I'm looking for warriors! I don't want chumps. You've got to destroy your opponents. This is war!"

Saber fencers have big mouths, Westbrook says. He uses his mouth to urge, coax, and praise his students. His aim is to make sure each kid knows that he or she has something special. These kids, he believes, are an untapped supply of fencing talent. They are already fighters. He and others at his Foundation will see to their training.

Each year, around thirty of the most promising Foundation students are invited to its after-school program. Here, they work one-on-one with coaches. The Foundation provides the equipment. When they are ready, students travel to competitions all over the world. The Foundation pays their expenses.

Great Support

The money for the equipment and travel expenses comes from Westbrook's fundraising efforts. Donors range from the United States Olympic Committee to the Philip Morris Corporation to Bill Cosby and Oprah Winfrey. Disney Studios has bought the film rights to his story. Students are required to chip in but never pay more than twenty dollars a year.

Students must keep their grades up. The Foundation finds tutors for them if they need help. Does it work? Here are a few results.

Students in a fencing class practice *thrust* and *parry* moves.

Herby Raynaud

Herby is ranked eighth in the country in saber for the 2003–2004 season. He sits on the Foundation's board of directors, coaches on Saturday mornings, and organizes the tutoring program. He began representing the Foundation at tournaments in 1996. He paid his own way.

Herby was born in New York to poor Haitian immigrants. His father died when Herby was very young. His mother's remarriage took them to a middle-class neighborhood in Brooklyn. Later, divorce landed them in tough Brooklyn neighborhoods. Herby fought when he had to. Usually, though, he used humor to ease situations.

Keeth Smart, Akhnaten Spencer-El, Patrick Durkam, and Herby Raynaud (left to right) come together to celebrate their success at the 2000 National Fencing Championships.

Herby was valedictorian—first—in his junior high school graduating class. So, he was selected for a program that took him to private prep schools. Like Westbrook, Herby felt that he had a foot in two worlds. He did not make the 2000 Olympic team. He wants to give it another try in the near future. He wants to stay in fencing, perhaps as a referee.

Akhnaten Spencer-El

Called "Akhi," Akhnaten Spencer-El is the first American fencer to achieve a number-one world ranking in his under-twenty division. He topped the under-twenty division in 1998, only six years into fencing. He won a gold medal at the Pan American games and was a 2000 Sydney Olympian. He has been offered a scholarship to St. John's University.

Akhi's mother urged him to take up fencing when he was fourteen. He did, but he had other problems and was in danger of flunking out of high school. Westbrook saw his ability and quick mind and stuck by him. Akhi says of the Foundation, "It's not just about fencing. It's a community."

Siblings Keeth and Erinn Smart

Keeth is the first American fencer to be ranked number one in the world. He was ranked number two at the 1998 and 1999 U.S. Nationals and is a two-time NCAA champion in saber. He competed in the 2000 Sydney Olympics. He attended St. John's University on a fencing scholarship with a major in finance.

Keeth Smart

Keeth's sister, Erinn Smart, is a National Champion in women's foil. She was a member of the U.S. Junior and Cadet World Team in 1997. She took fifth place in the 1997 World Cadet Championships. She won the bronze at the 1997 Junior World Cup in Dourdan, France. She was an alternate at the 2000 Sydney Olympics. She attends Barnard College, the women's college at Columbia University.

Erinn Smart

Keeth and Erinn grew up in Flatbush, an area in Brooklyn, New York. Their mother is Jamaican; their father is African American. One of the family rules was that bad grades meant no fencing. The same rule applies at the Foundation: "No pass, no play."

The Smarts came to fencing when their father read a newspaper article about the Westbrook Foundation. The kids were there on the very first Saturday morning. Erinn, 11, took to the sport right away. Keeth became serious about it a few months later. When he saw how good his sister was, sibling rivalry kicked in. Many years later, they continue to support each other.

Harvey Miller

Harvey was a United States Junior Olympic Champion just eighteen months after he first picked up a saber.

An African American, he is from Queens, New York. During his sophomore year of high school, he failed every class except physical education. He came to fencing at age eighteen, after his mother heard a radio show about Westbrook's Foundation. She sat Harvey down and said, "It's boot camp or fencing. Choose."

Harvey watched a Saturday morning exhibition bout between Keeth Smart and Akhi Spencer-El. He saw their speed and gracefulness. The next Saturday, he fought a practice saber bout against a boy ranked eleventh in the country in his age group. Harvey won. He next defeated an older fencer. He was hooked.

Harvey Miller fences four afternoons a week and on Saturdays. He made his high school's honor roll. He went to night school to make up the courses he had failed. He took an SAT preparatory class and attends St. John's University, majoring in computer science. He wants to earn a master's degree in it.

Looking to the Future

The Peter Westbrook Foundation is training some of the top-ranked fencers in the country. Westbrook says his future Olympic teams are coming along and show a lot of promise.

Fencers ready? Westbrook's warriors are ready, and they are hungry! So, as they have said many times before and will say many times again, "Bring on the sword!"

Members of the 2004 U.S. Olympic Fencing Team—
Erinn Smart, Keeth Smart, Peter Westbrook, Ivan Lee,
Tim Morehouse (left to right)